CHARLEY HARPER

SKETCHBOOK

HOW TO DRAW
28 BIRDS
in HARPER'S STYLE

Pomegranate Communications, Inc.
19018 NE Portal Way, Portland, OR 97230
800-227-1428   www.pomegranate.com

Pomegranate Europe
Number 3 Siskin Drive, Middlemarch Business Park
Coventry, CV3 4FJ, UK
+44 (0)24 7621 4461   sales@pomegranate.com

Item No. AA785

Designed by Stephanie Odeh
Printed in Korea

28 27 26 25 24 23 22 21 20 19   12 11 10 9 8 7 6 5 4 3

AN avid naturalist, Charley Harper particularly liked to paint birds. He masterfully portrayed a host of species using simple lines and shapes. From the smallest songbird to the largest seabird, Harper conveyed not only the form and coloration of his avian subjects but also their personalities. His minimalist approach did not reduce the impact of his art; instead, it offered a bold and unique interpretation of nature's winged beauties.

This sketchbook gives you the opportunity to learn how Harper captured his subjects with the fewest possible visual elements. For each of the twenty-eight birds featured herein, we've included a four-page presentation. On the first page, you will find line drawings that show a three-stage process for recreating Harper's image. The line drawings build on each other: the first one presents the most basic shapes, the second further develops the form of the bird, and the third completes the image with all the details. Following the line drawings are two uncoated sheets on which you can mimic these lines and shapes. Harper's original full-color bird image completes each sequence. The sketchbook progresses from the simpler of Harper's bird images to the more complex. In some cases, the line drawings present a slightly modified version of the original art.

At the end of the book, you will find thirty pages for your continued sketching, be it using Harper's style or your own bold and unique approach. Happy bird sketching!

Wildlife artist Charley Harper (American, 1922–2007) came by his love of nature as a child growing up in rural West Virginia. After studying at the Art Academy of Cincinnati and the Art Students League in New York City, he gained acclaim as a commercial illustrator for numerous publications, most notably *The Golden Book of Biology* and *Animal Kingdom,* published in the 1960s. As demand for his work grew, he went on to have a successful business producing limited-edition silkscreen prints.

A supporter of many ecological causes, Harper designed over fifty posters for national and international conservation organizations, as well as many national parks, nature centers, zoological gardens, and government agencies. His iconic posters celebrate biodiversity and express concern for the plight of animals and birds subject to habitat destruction and other environmental problems. Among his most famous posters are those he created for the US National Park Service and the Monteverde Cloud Forest Preserve in Costa Rica.

Harper became famous for depicting birds and other wildlife using combinations of simple shapes. Instead of drawing small details, he captured a critter's character by reducing its form down to the most easily recognized features—the big bill of a pelican, for example, or the tall tail of a roadrunner. Describing this method, Harper once said, "When I look at a wildlife or nature subject, I don't see the feathers in the wings; I just count the wings." He asked viewers to "remember that I didn't start out to paint a bird—the bird already existed. I started out to paint a picture of a bird, a picture which didn't exist before I came along, a picture which gives me a chance to share with you my thoughts about the bird."

Pomegranate publishes many products featuring Charley Harper's art—from calendars, jigsaw puzzles, sticker kits, and playing cards to notecards, postcards, invitations, and gift wrap. In 2013 Pomegranate launched a series of Charley Harper Nature Discovery Books; the first book in the series, titled *What's in the Woods?,* offers a unique opportunity to learn about nature and to examine how an artist interprets its details, beauty, and wonder.

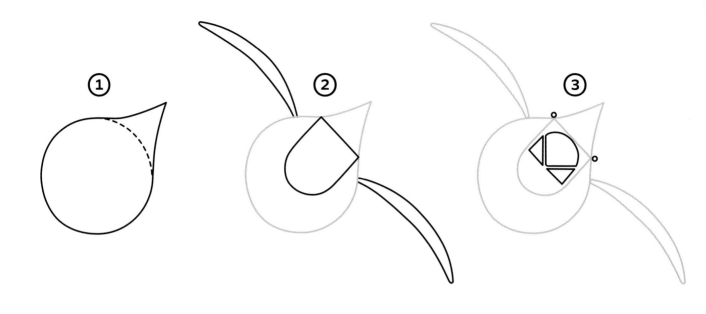

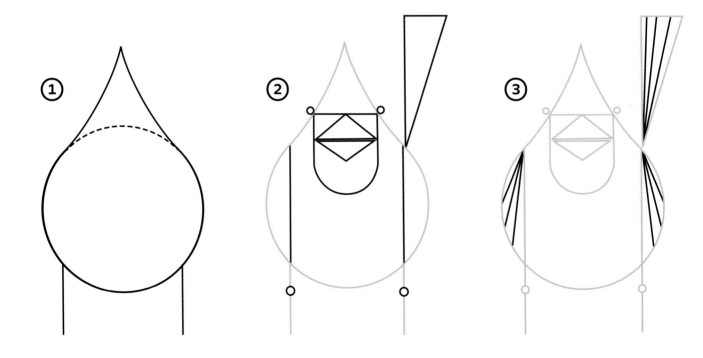

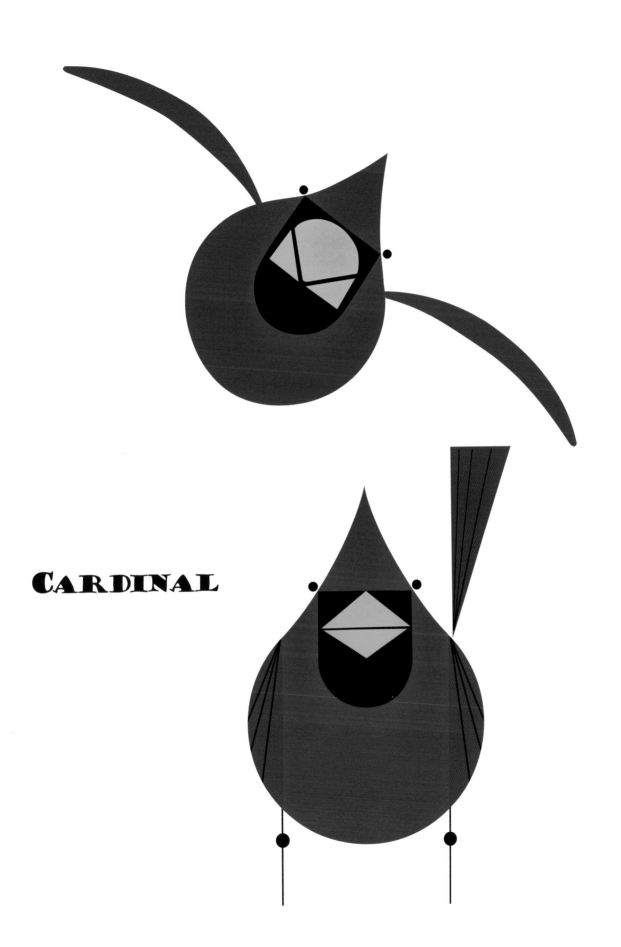

CARDINAL

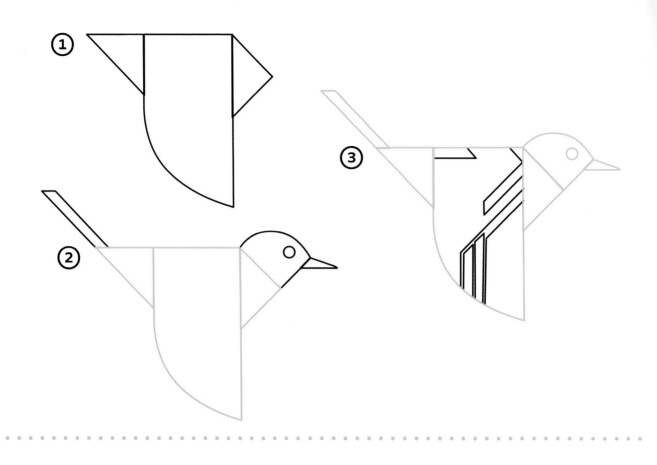

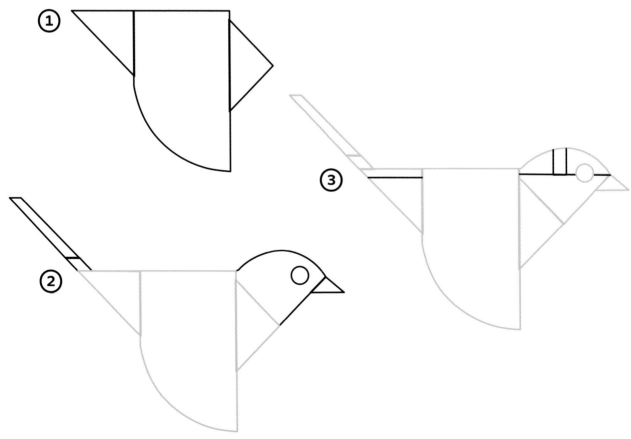

WESTERN TANAGER

GOULDIAN FINCH

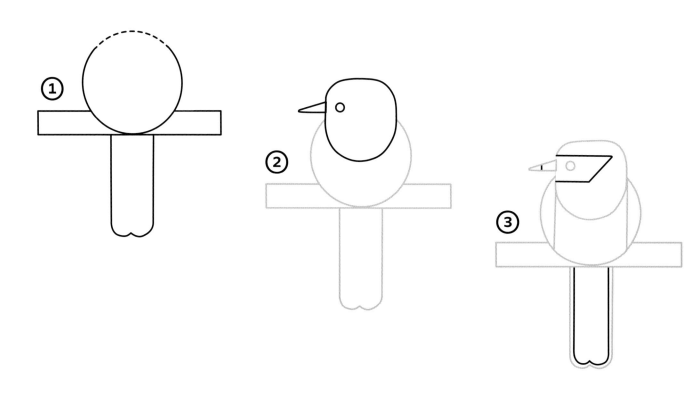

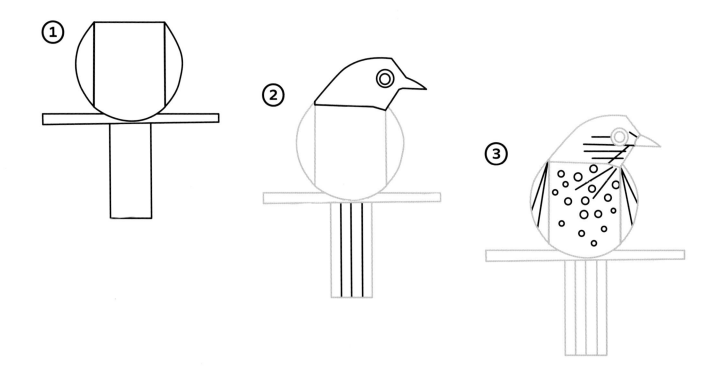

WARBLER

WOOD THRUSH

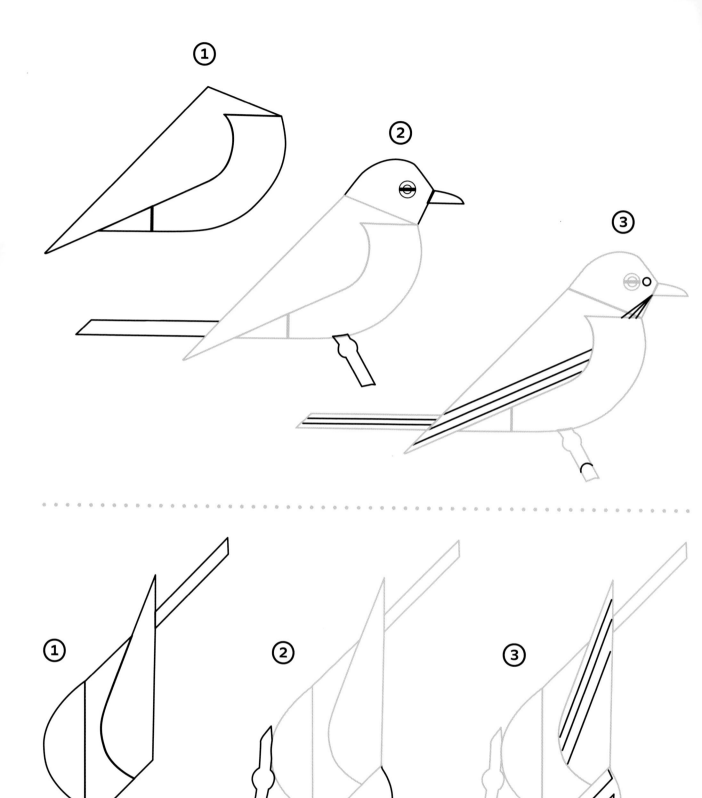

AMERICAN
ROBIN

MOUNTAIN
CHICKADEE

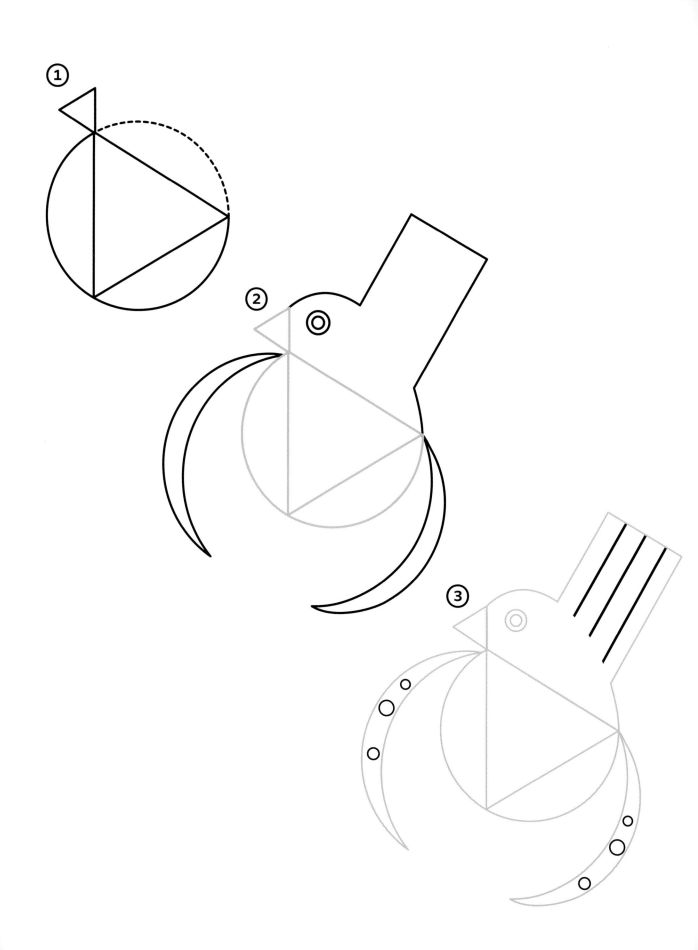

ROSE–BREASTED GROSBEAK

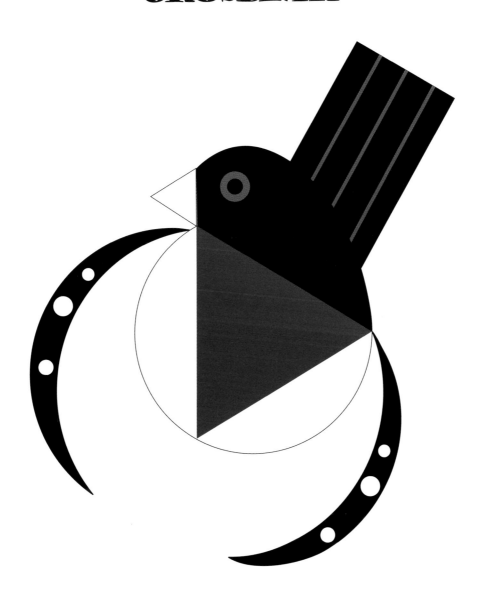

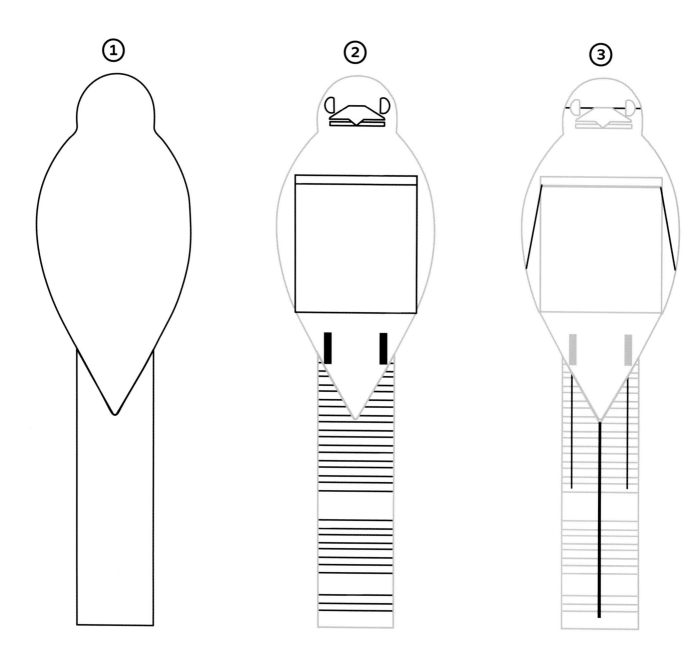

ORANGE-BELLIED TROGON

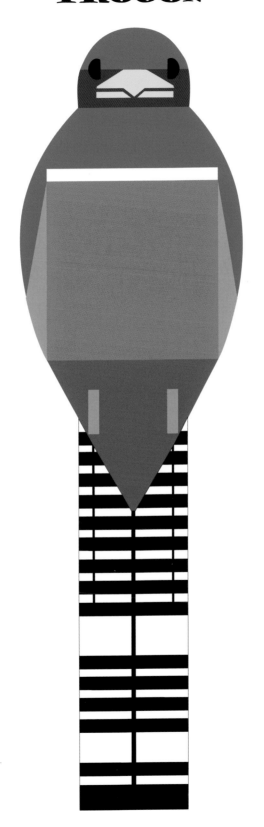

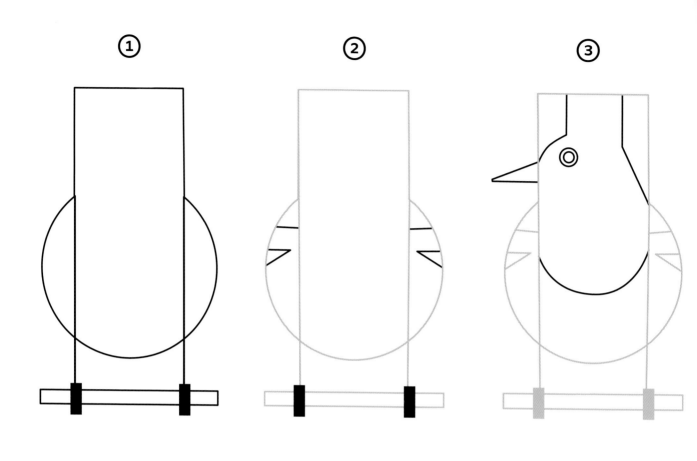

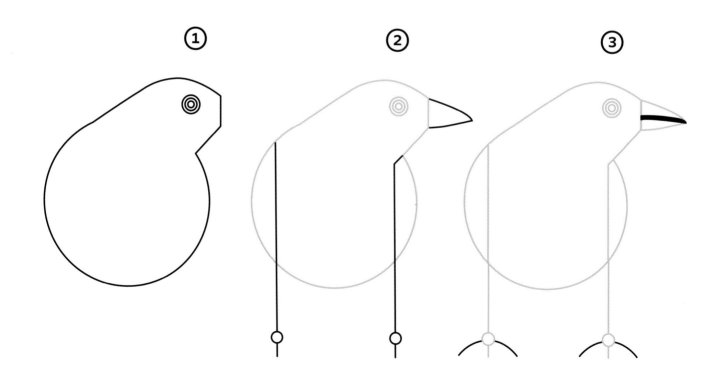

BALTIMORE ORIOLE

FINCH

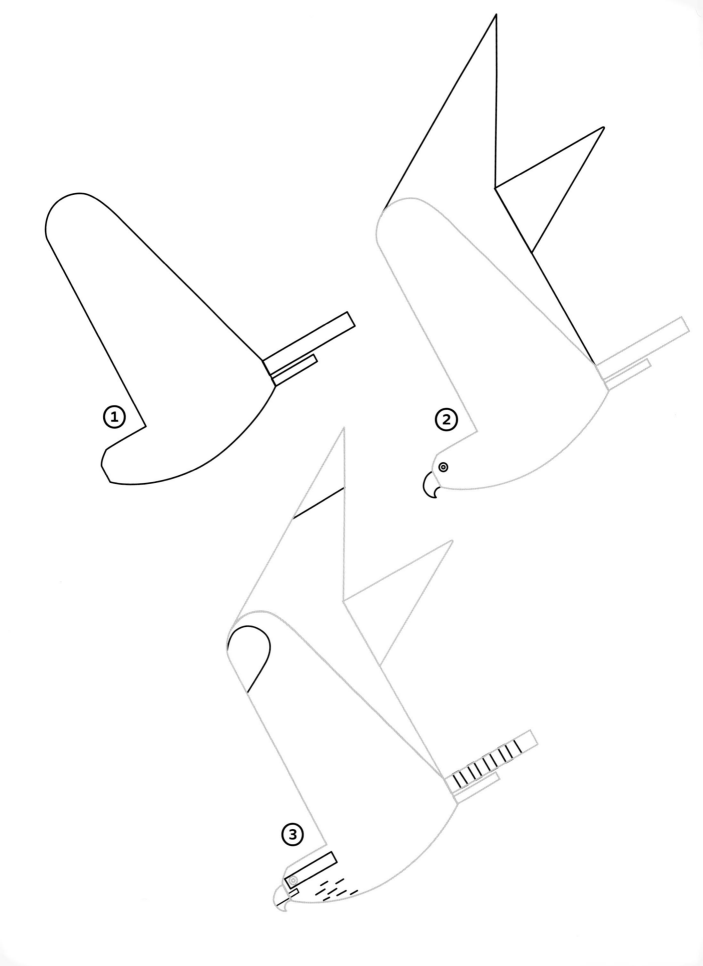

OSPREY

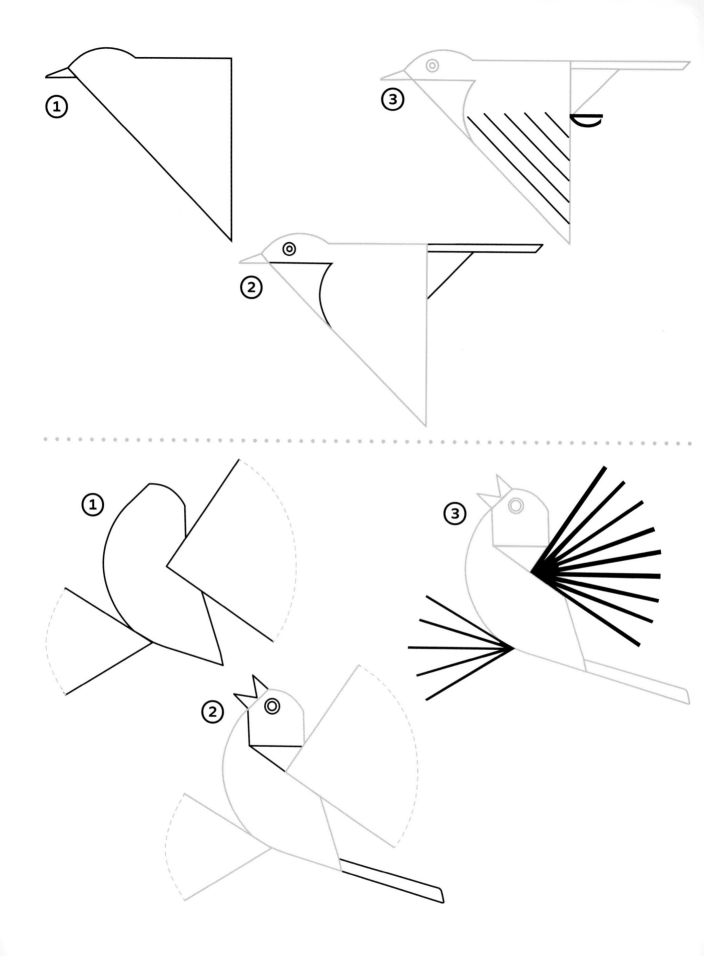

EASTERN BLUEBIRD

PAINTED BUNTING

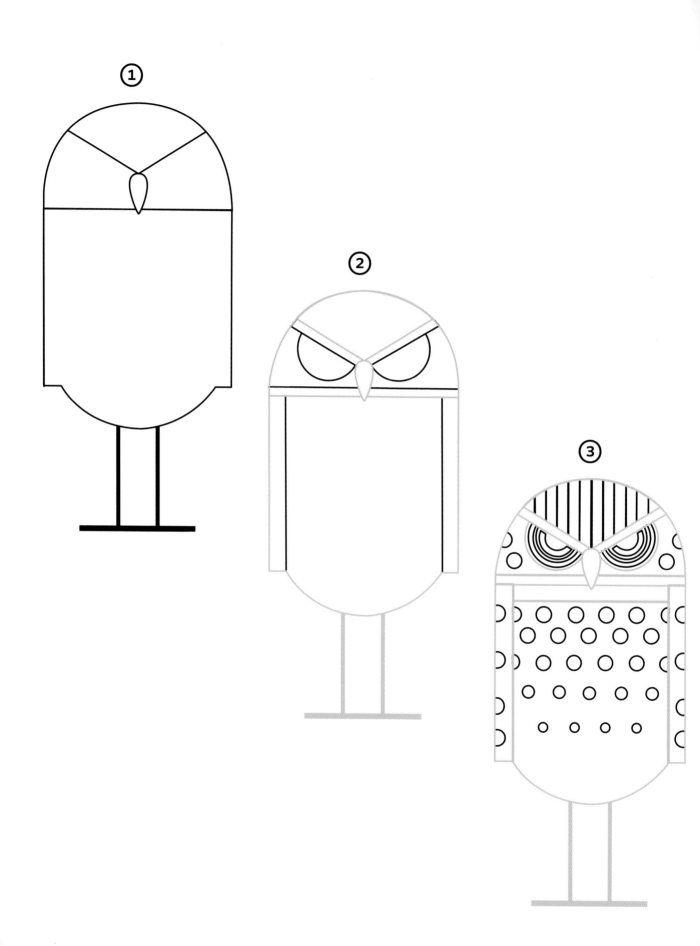

BURROWING OWL

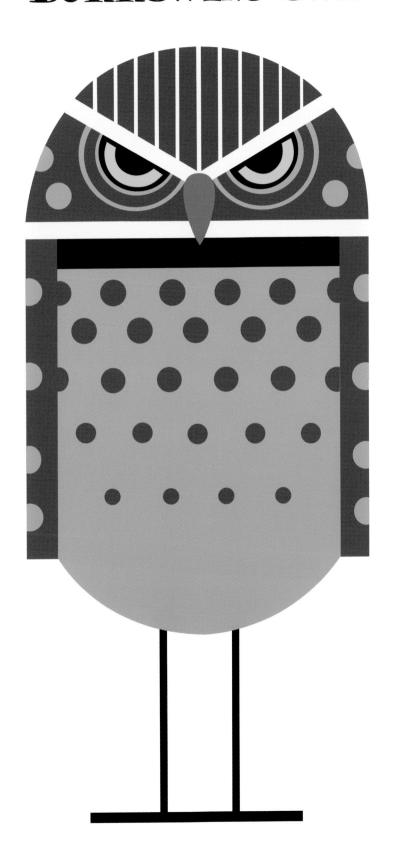

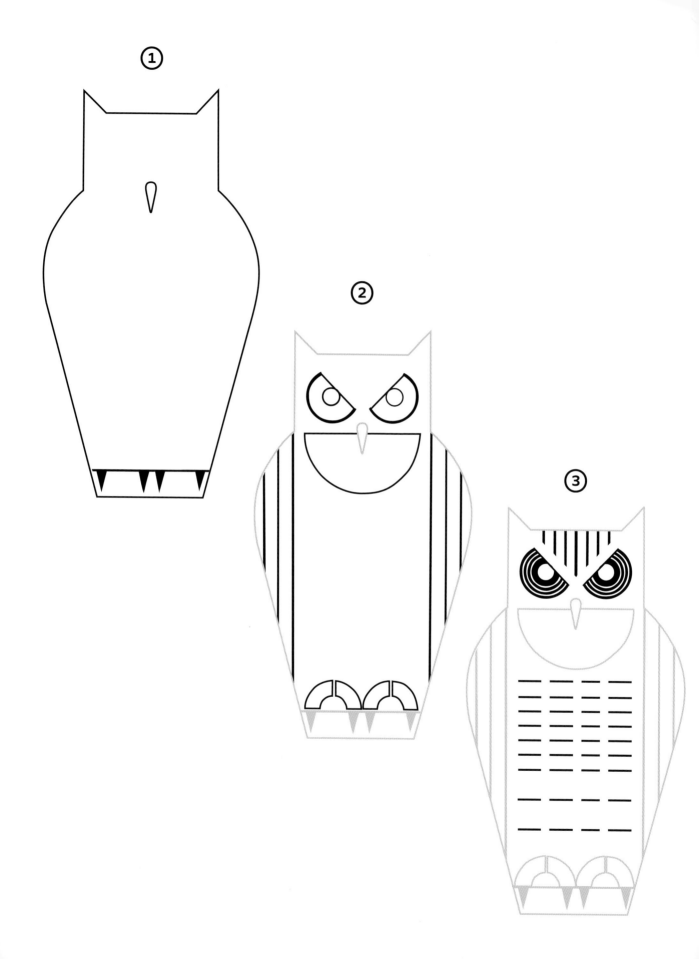

GREAT HORNED OWL

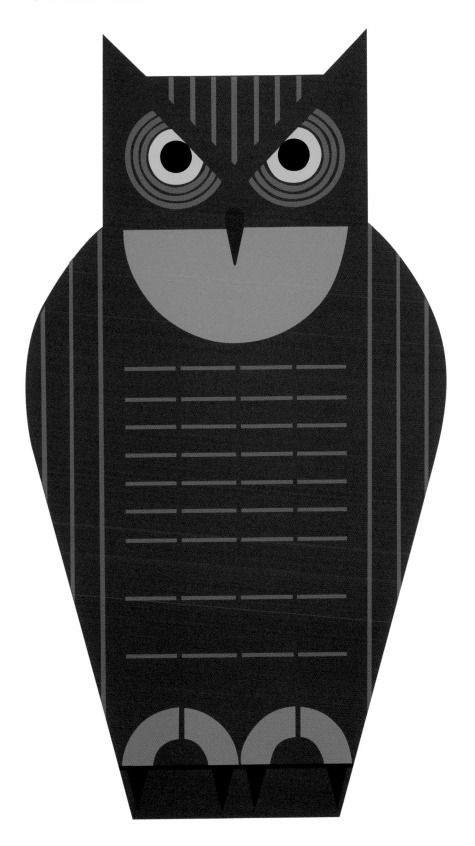

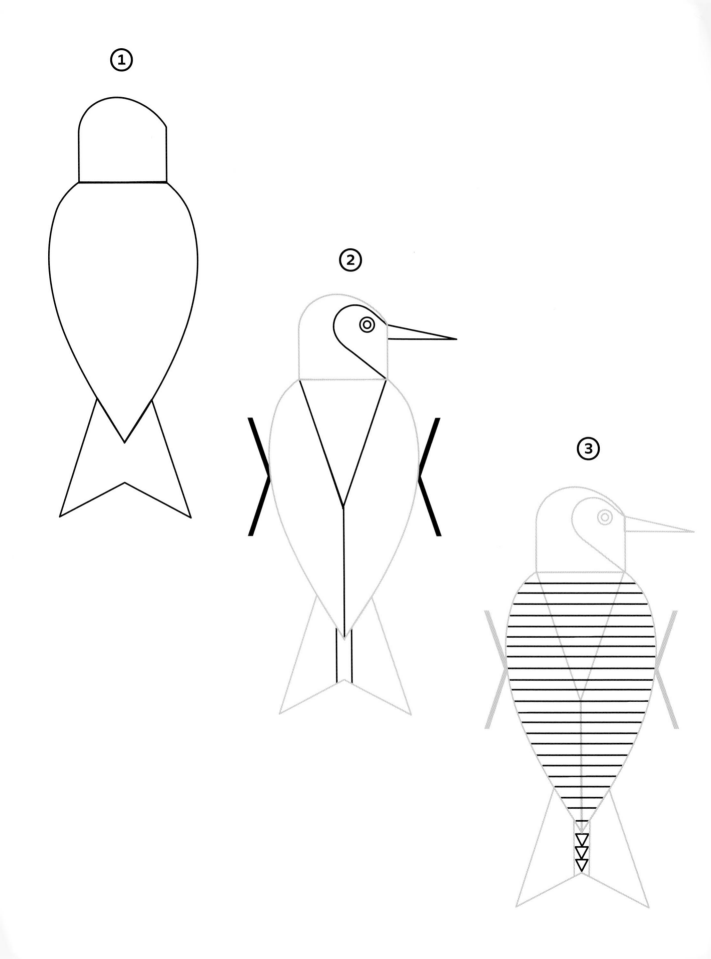

RED-BELLIED WOODPECKER

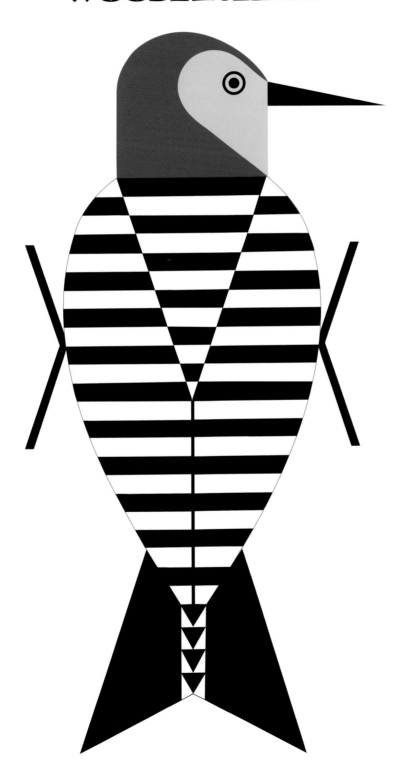

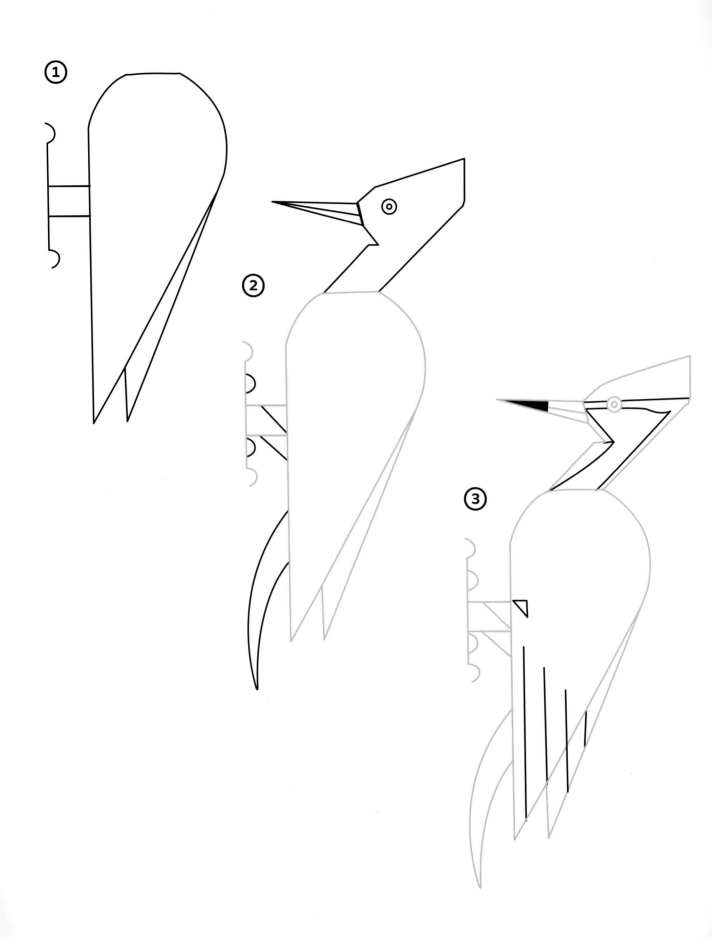

PILEATED WOODPECKER

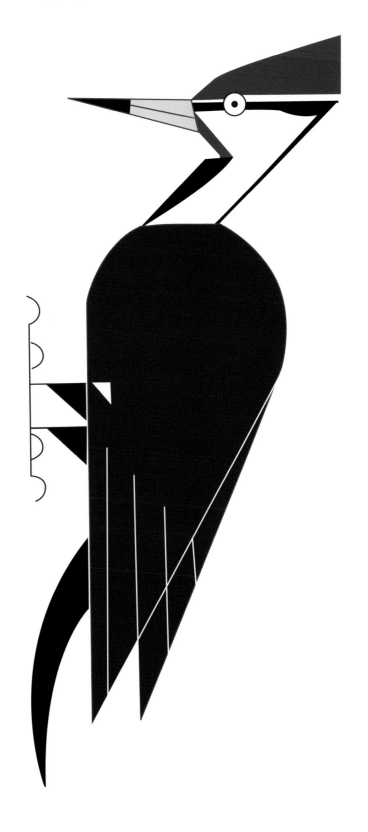

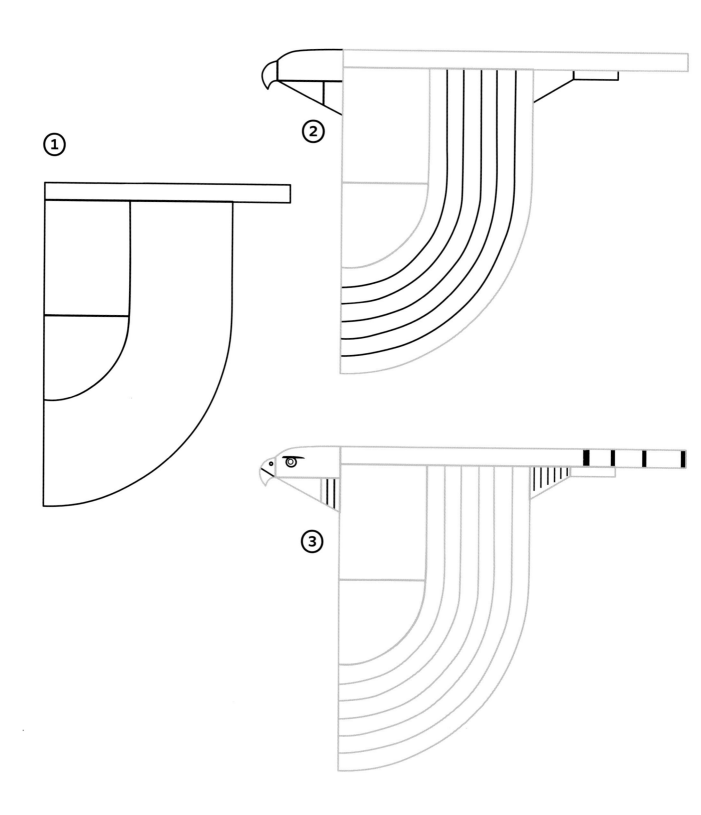

FALCON

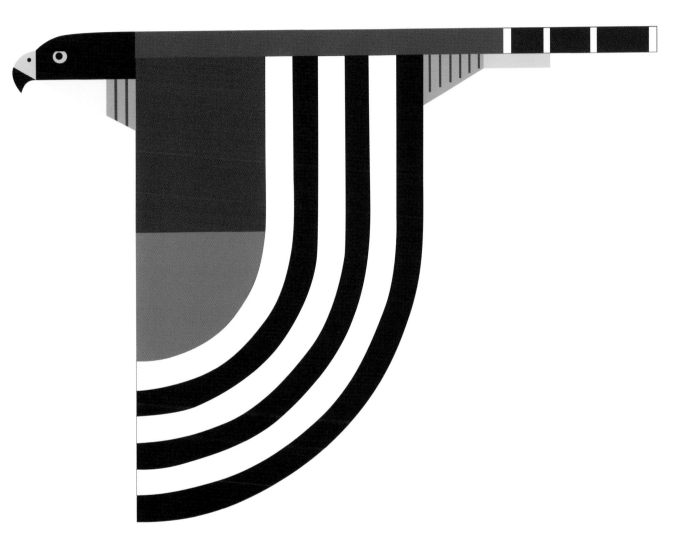

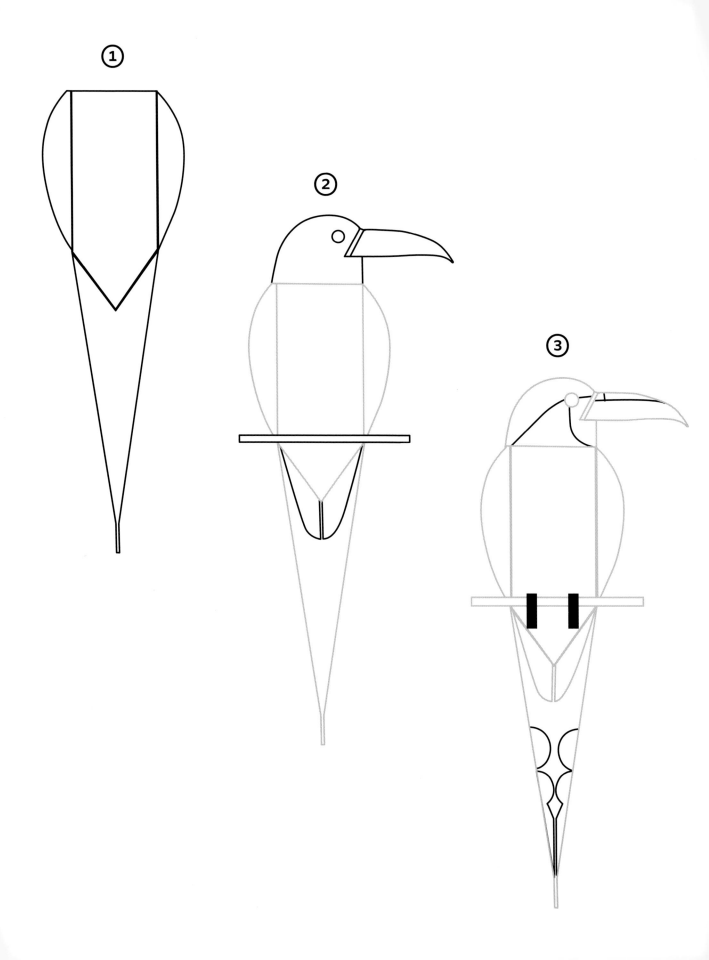

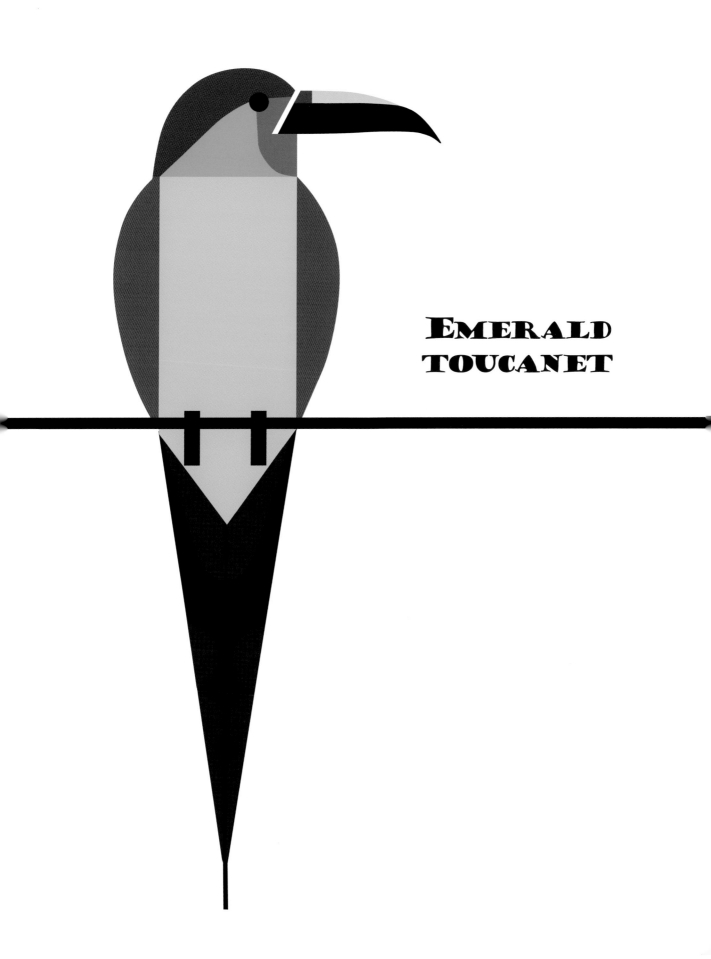

EMERALD
TOUCANET

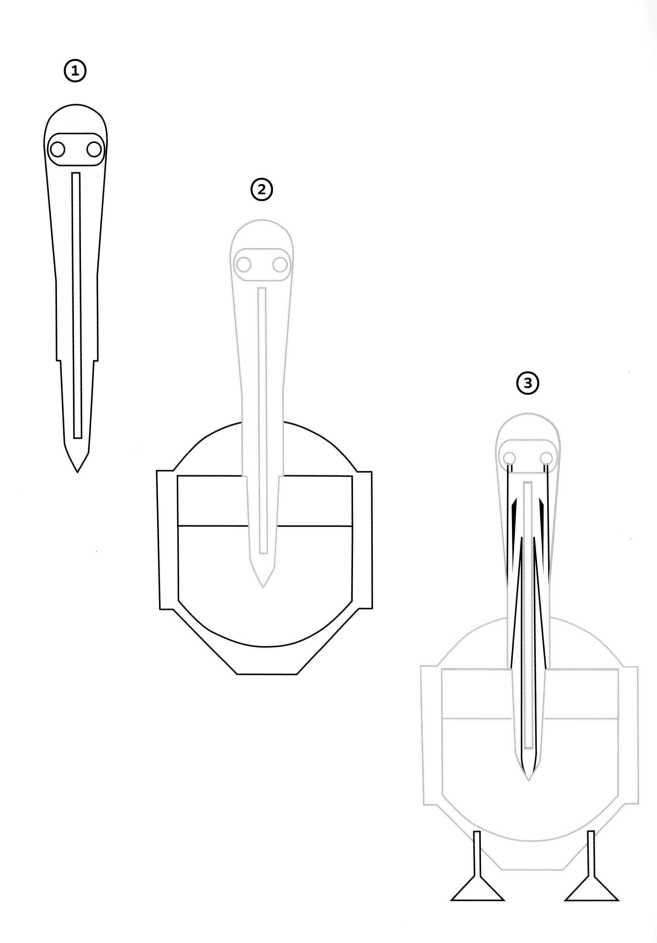

PELICAN

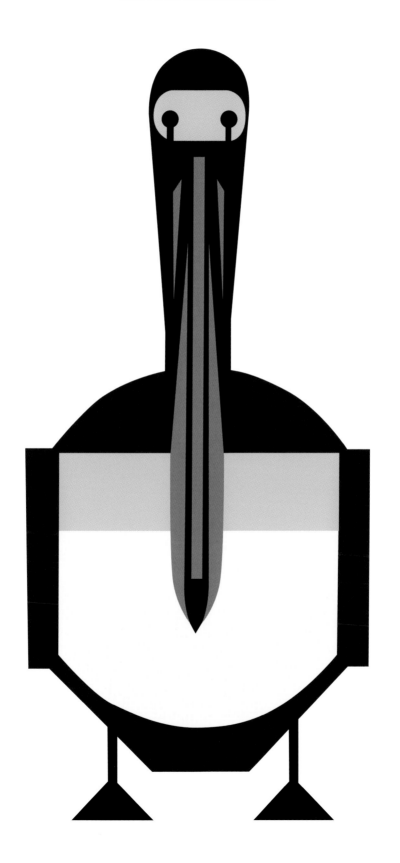

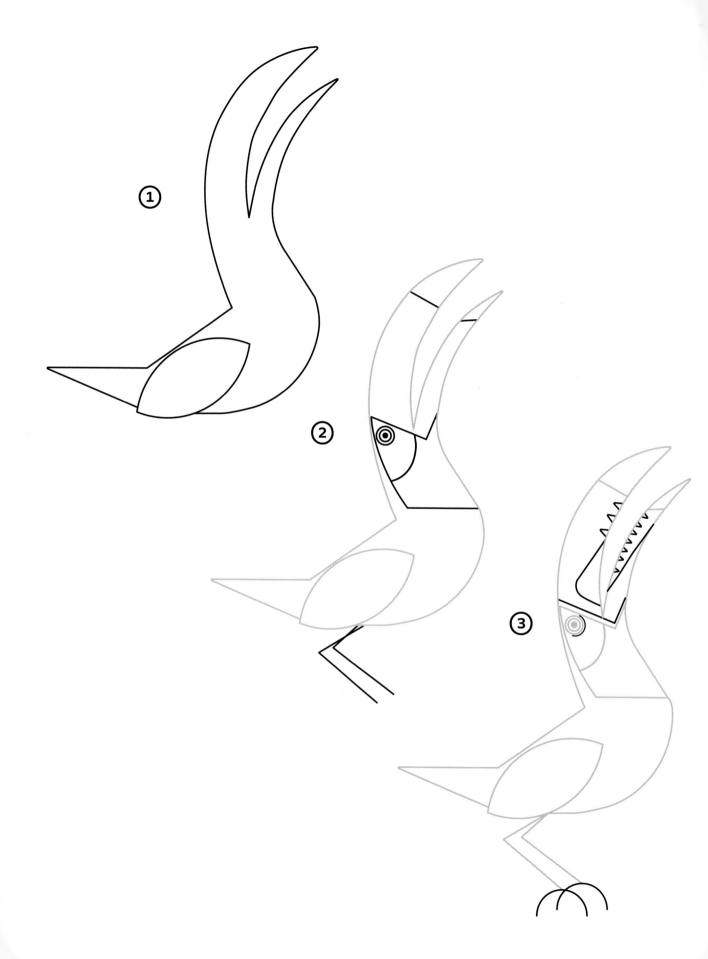

KEEL-BILLED
TOUCAN

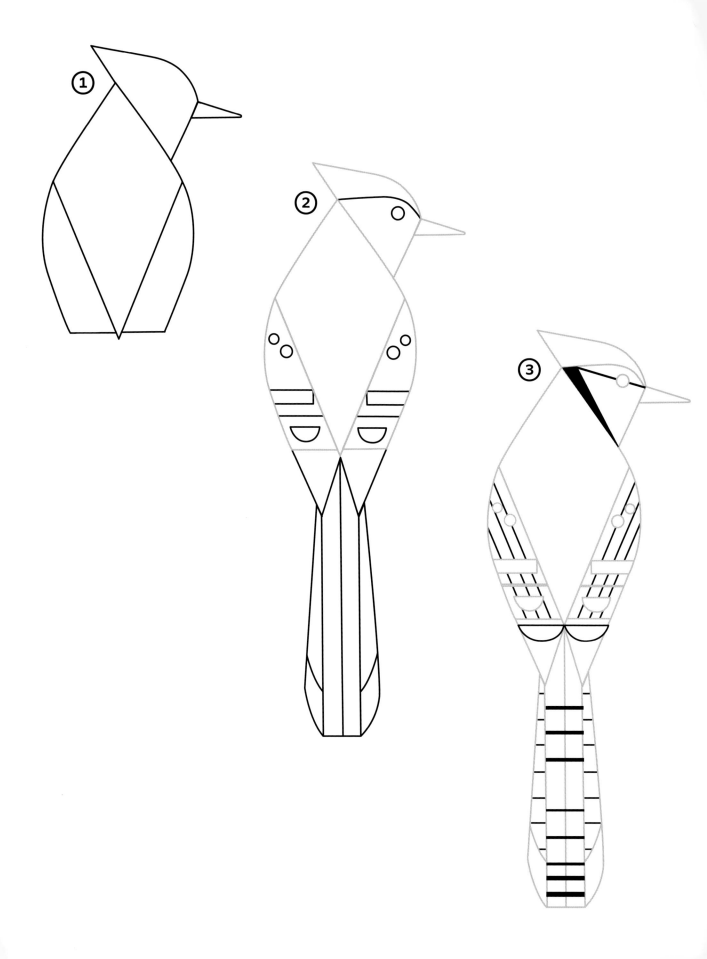

BLUE JAY

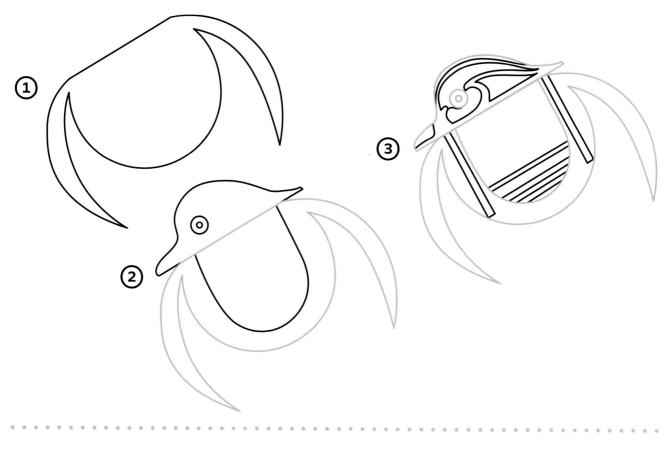

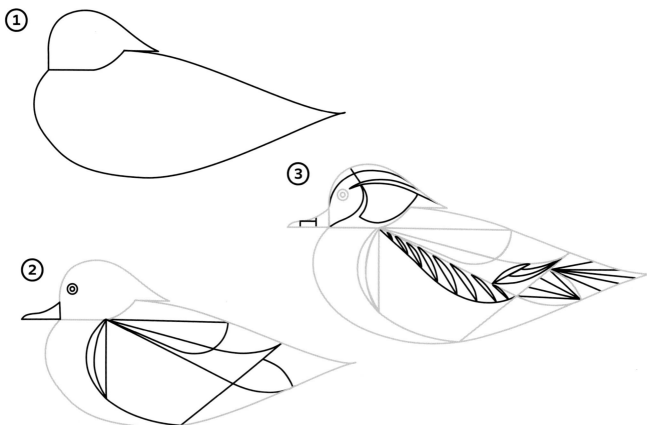

WOOD DUCK

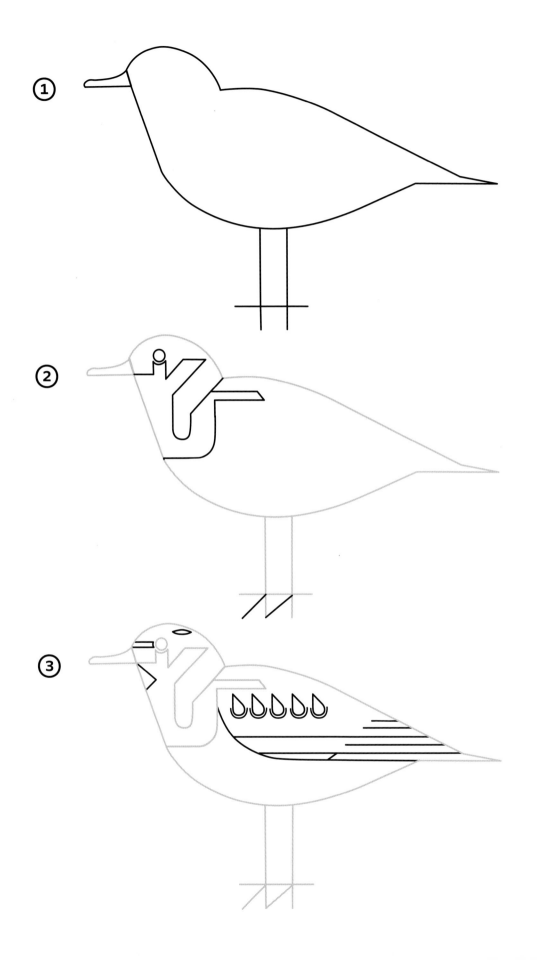

RUDDY TURNSTONE

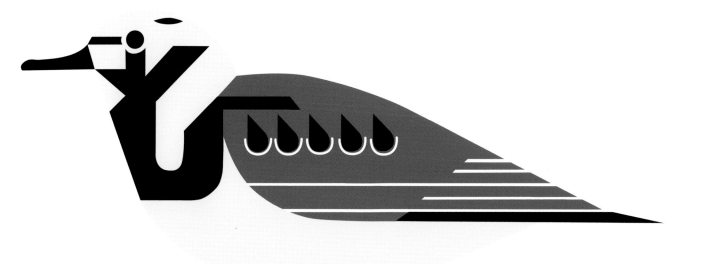
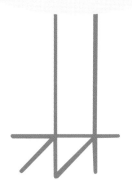

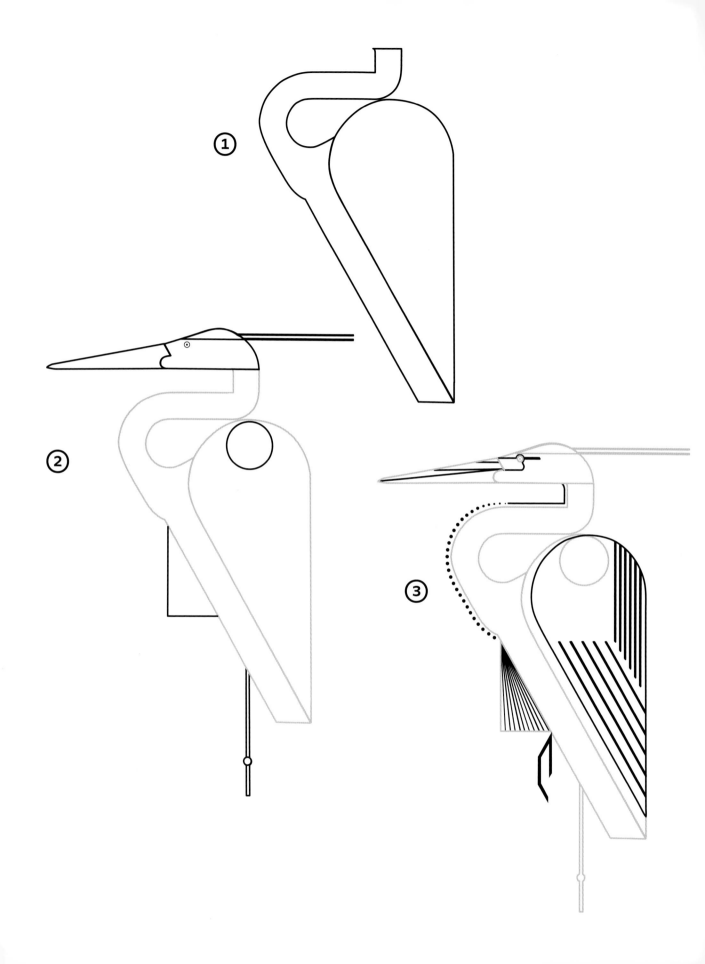

GREAT BLUE HERON

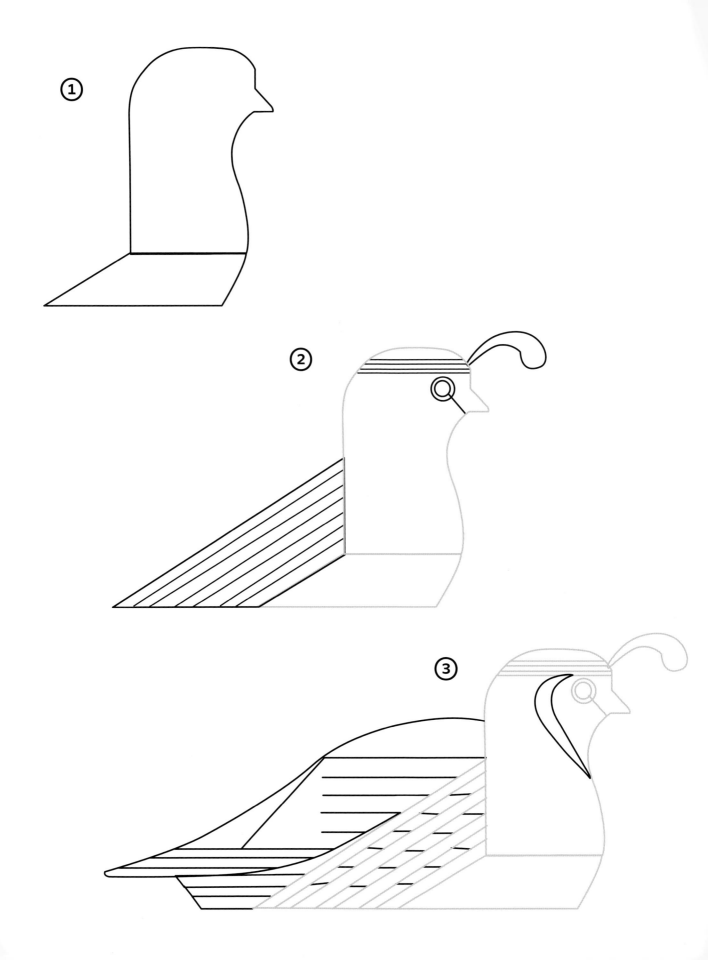

CALIFORNIA
QUAIL

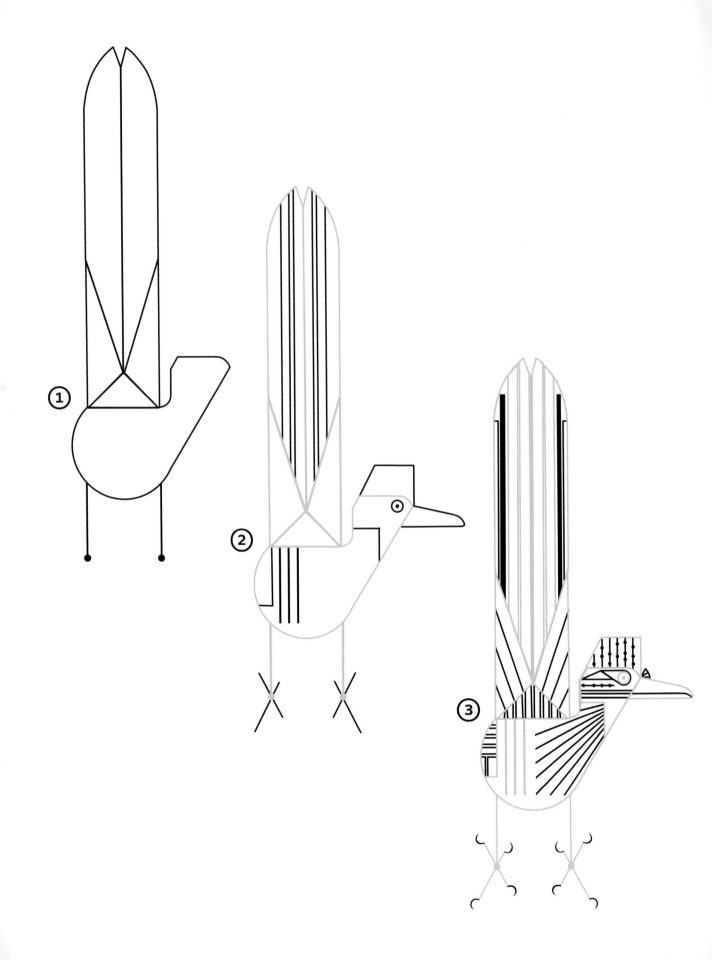

ROADRUNNER